Ruah

A Journal of Spiritual Poetry

Address correspondence to:
Power of Poetry - *A Celebration*
c/o Dominican School of Philosophy and Theology
2401 Ridge Rd.
Berkeley, CA 94709
E-mail: cjrenzop@yahoo.com
www.popruah.org

Power of Poetry is a membership organization affiliated with the Dominican
School of Philosophy and Theology. Please help us with a donation or a
membership in Power of Poetry ($10.00 annually, includes a copy of *Ruah*).
Make checks payable to Power of Poetry/DSPT.

Special thanks to our anonymous benefactors. We could not continue without
them!

Ruah: A Journal of Spiritual Poetry, Vol. XIV (2004) © 2004 by
Power of Poetry - *A Celebration*, Berkeley, CA.

Acknowledgments by Charles Wright: "Jesuit Graves," in *Black Zodiac* (New
York: The Noonday Press, 1997); "A Short History of the Shadow," "Thinking of
Marsillo Ficino at the First Hint of Autumn," and "Via Negativa," in *A Short
History of the Shadow* (New York: Farrar, Straus & Giroux, 2002); "There is a
Balm in Gilead," and "Homage to Mark Rothko," in *Buffalo Yoga* (New York:
Farrar, Straus & Giroux, 2004).

Acknowledgments by Edward Dougherty: "Setting Out" and Opening," in
Friends Journal; "A Roomful of Expectation," in *manna*; "Into Darkness," in
Poetry East; "The Craft Studio," in *Whetstone*; and "Fireflies in Bamboo Grove,"
"Woodchip Path," and "How Ants Felled Two Trees," in *Parting Gifts*.

Cover Artwork: © by Siger Köder, "Elija am Horeb."

ISSN 1072-4524
ISBN 1-88-3734-14-2

Ruah

Volume XIV

Power of Poetry — *A Celebration*
BERKELEY, CALIFORNIA
2004

Contents

        Winner of the 2004 *New Eden Chapbook Competition*

Editor's Preface

I've been doing a bit of thinking lately about the general nature of prayer. I mean what is it, *really*!?

Perhaps each of us would have a different answer; and each answer would be, somehow, "correct." Nevertheless, there has to be some kind of common element(s) to this activity, or thing, we call "prayer."

From my own experience and that of the people to whom I minister, I have come to know prayer as the establishment of *real* relationships between the subject (pray-er), God, and the "object" (whether it be a person, place, or thing). Prayer is not simply a two-way activity, between myself and God. It also draws a third party (even if only myself) into a dynamic encounter.

Most importantly, the relationships established through prayer are real. They are not simply symbolic, but dynamic, engaging and life-changing! When human persons are involved, prayer becomes a meeting place, with God as the host. Healing is possible through prayer when two people willingly enter God's space, *together*.

I mention all of this because I believe poetry functions in a similar way. As with prayers, poems set up real relationship between the subject (poet), the Transcendent (God, for the believer), and the "object" (reader). And, as with prayer, these relationships are real, *very* real, indeed!

Jaques Maritain speaks about this functioning in terms of the capacity of poetry to impart connatural (or intuitive) knowledge. Though different than speculative knowledge (the kind generated by science), it is nevertheless *real* knowledge! Every poet uses words to set up a place where others may encounter the Transcendent. Yet, in so doing, the poet allows us to encounter one another, and in a way which transforms everyone.

But you don't have to take my word. Just read the poems found here in *Volume XIV*. They will speak on my behalf.

In this season of great global strife, the poets of *Vol. XIV* offer us a meeting place for peace and healing. As Elijah before the mouth of the cave at Mt. Horeb, may we too hear the voice of God and be forever changed. . . .

Let the celebration begin!

C. J. Renz, O.P.

Waking

Kate Martin

Whatever wakes me these days
wakes me early.
Crickets trill drowsily
at the remaining darkness;
traffic begins to make its claim
on the edges of night.

The house is heavy with silence
as I pace from room to room;
dreams and disproportionate fears recede,
concerns for the day ahead
come alert, ready for trouble.

Too late for sleep, too early for tasks,
this is a time to sit in the faltering dark
and watch the shape of my life
emerge from the night
like the trees, the pale flowers,
the windows lighting up one by one.

Ambush

Michael E. Stone

God lies in wait in the intervals,
Between intrusions of us,
Between every and day,
Between now and then.

It's easy not to see intervals,
To miss God's ambush,
To avoid the one glimpsed
Out of the eye's corner.

Satan, they say,
Resides in the details:
The Nazi clerk
Listing transports.

Needlework
Margarita Engle

He wore no thimble
while embroidering stars
moon and sun
in the night sky.

The pain of pierced fingers
was diligent practice
for later wounds
palm and foot
forehead, side.

A decision was made.
All creatures created in His image
would receive partial thimbles
hard, smooth natural coverings
on the upper surface of fingers
and toes, moon-marked nails
to encourage the stitching
of patchwork repairs
both useful land decorative
in the delicate fabric
of life's daily
nights.

Vow

Janet McCann

the word itself
solemn and chagrined,
i promise not to,
i give up, abjure,
i will never. if broken
a permanent break
a tear in the fabric,
unhealable. if kept
a backpack each day
growing heavier, the fine
silt of time, almost
invisible but not
quite, graying
everything. the back
aches but you shift
the load, a little
proud to shoulder it,
so that some day
you can think,
i didn't, i never
even really wanted to.

Eve & Mary

Chet Corey

Eve drew onto herself the opened hand of Adam,
formed it round the face-like curve of reddened fruit,
as she had found his favored hand that night,
had drawn its unfamiliar fingers, its awkward thumb,
along each numbered rib and up to pluck
the budding blossom of her engorged breast.
It would be again as in their wedding bed,
his breathing lifting like the wind her auburn hair;
and Adam would come to know what she had known.

Just so, behind the grate where Cana's women stood,
his mother saw him enter unannounced, to take his place
among its men, his entourage as numbered as the groom's.
Her eyes spoke, as her mothering eyes had spoken into his
when she would move him to her other breast.
And his reply was much the same: What did Jesus know
of emptiness and time, his hour come fully round,
as once had hers—she pushing out, the steward at his side,
asking, like Mary's angel, what it was she would have done.

The Drying Time

Annabelle Moseley

In the silence that comes after a storm,
She confronts
Her deepest prayers,
The ones she carefully buried—
The rain has caused them to emerge,
Smelling like old pennies
Pressed in a tightened hand.
They tap against the gutter
And ask to be heard.

This is the time before the rush of day,
Before the alarm and coffee sounds,
Before the traffic and commute.
This is when
She hears
Her breathing
As the rain runs off the roof.

Somewhere in that drying time, she sleeps—
Until morning lights her prayers again,
And God licks the dew
Off their copper backs,
And listens.

In Memoriam
Vietnam Memorial

David Napolin

The trees are stiletto forms
in the clean moonlight.
Cold and pale they harken back to soldier kind:
shadows of men who stand
and line the ground,
as with the air cool and fine
memories of them.

They bore the essence of this moonlight
when they crossed the sea to do their chores:
and these firm stationed boughs
beautiful as courage
keep their spirit here.

As the branch slits the light
and breaks the sky
so their arms were raised in high gesture,
and if they failed
a noble sky still holds their glory here
and stays for us to look upon.

Telephone Lines

Alexander Levering Kern

Inside the picture frame
formed by your window
pane you see tiny twig
fingers tickling the slate
grey sky, coaxing laughter
from a sullen day.
Wrapped among three
slender wires shines a silver form.
You blink and see a cross
holding three as one
in streetlit mystery,
and you wonder: what words
of love must course
through these lines,
electric and complete?

Rock of Massabielle

Sharon Mollerus

A cascade of candles huddled
like the pilgrims who lean into the sloping stone
for shelter against a weeping wind.
The pearly tapers in a wax pyramid
whisper their prayers and burn down to spongy stubs.

A slanting rain foams over the loosened earth;
severed grass roots and softening clay clumps
ooze down the embankments of the river,
a roiling rust, a melting world.
Dust to dust.

I bow my head under a leaf green umbrella,
holding it low against the gusts which try to capsize it.
My rubber-bottom cane glides in front of me
along the slipper marble floor. I dare not fall—
alone across the ocean from home.
An icy blast whistles through the peaks of the Pyrenees
and ducks beneath the cheap chiffon scarf
with the imprinted basilica tied under my chin—
the one I bought from an old lady in black,
a widow like me, on an inclined sidewalk
across from the cemetery.

Lady at the rock who waited for Bernadette,
asthmatic child sleeping in a stone jail.
She met her at Massabielle, this rock
I touch while icy water seeps
in rivulets down the blackened crevices.
She waits to meet me now—
will my daughter have Mass said over me?—
now and at a time soon.
Ashes to ashes.

Fugue

Meghan Nuttall Sayres

Wind devils
awaken firs,

barn swallows flip
between raindrops,

and mice
scuttle under hay.

Here, I
sometimes hear

coyotes yip,
and see beyond where

the moonlight
fades. Alfalfa

glistens
like lucky shillings

in starlight;
and the wool

of my sheep
shines on the hoof

as if something holy
lives in it.

Night Out

B. Z. Niditch

This scoured night
has injured love
even the moon is forgetful
and marble stars
are dull in the dark sky

My grandmother used
to speak of such heavens
in another tongue
but who paid any mind
for phantoms or prophecies

What sanctuary Hamlet
imposes its ghost
a watermark of fever
on the brooding darkness

When You've Become the Star
Daniel Mills

Not once has thawing snow
turned coldly on the sun
with epithets like:

"Hot-blooded Murder!"
or "Destroyer of My
Shining Brilliance!"

When you've become the star
you're looking at, what else can you do
but blaze and melt?

Fall, again and again,
like some heaven-heady jewel
from the very heights of love.

going forward

Peter Layton

I don't sing to single you out
my throat booming the outcast throwaway lines
the lines from songs too hard to remember
I was always getting it wrong
not getting the whole point
like pointing my auto to some distant point
where all of the so-called reality meets at a vortex

I was amazed you could learn to
collapse, collide everything
in creation
the teacher said this, this is the vanishing point
pointing to it
all the pencil lines drawn straight edge sharp
to it

and knowing everything
all the trains both real and imagined
all the roads
hurtling toward that final dot
which showed itself quickly if you looked
on the television's cathode tube
and closed the same as a closing sad eye

or a last mouth
emptied now of its secrets, its warmth
at the frightening end of sentences

Drinking the Bowl of Bhakti

Tara Moghadam

I was only there to wash his feet
the silver bowl a liquid moon on the floor between us

he lay on his back
eyes closed, one arm
draped across his brow

christmas lights traced
the beams across the ceiling
we were not alone

I lifted one foot from the floor
guided it into the warm water
cupping my hands
I began to bathe the ankle

perhaps I thought, *I will give you all I can*
perhaps I thought, *I will heal all I can*

I do not remember thinking

I remember white skin
the taut tendon at the waist of the ankle
the heel worn smooth as river stone

my thumbs pressing just
beneath the ball of the foot
as if I were opening a peach
ready to watch it split in perfect halves

the water trickled like juice from my fingers

neither of us knew what
would come to sit on us
this a sheet of rain

we took on as a sheen
wet streets beneath the lamplight

my eyes were closed
the air we breathed
swollen with memory

neither of us knew how to
read the ancient red stone
the blood of meaning, our souls
carved into the canyon walls
wood smoke and river water
my clay hands coloring the sky

I am sure I thought
I will give you all I can
I will heal all I can

but this is something so different from thinking

these places we are born
the palm of my hand
always cradles your heel
lifting your foot from the water
to brush you dry

I move so slowly now
when I kiss the clean slope of your oiled foot
there is no part of us unknown

what hovers here is
too big for humans to hold

tomorrow you'll pass it along
forehead to the ground
bowed to a friend

Thursday

Holly Day

it's raining again and I
can smell the barbecue pit next door
flooding out onto
the lawn. Age

spoils even this
early morning storm—I am so tired
of being a human
barometer

head pounds as clouds collapse, release
joints sigh in relief as
the first drops fall

birds chirp crazy outside
I can even smell the grass growing.

Bill

Sue Spirit

Propped up on six pillows
to breathe
I inhale *Field and Stream*—
    shining trout leaping narrows
    moose ambling my dreams.
Some hate me for that UPS heist I pulled
but that was then:
some believe in me again.
I catch frogs with balls of lard,
lure snapping turtles from their dens.
I can load up with the best of them
at a Chinese buffet:
    spring rolls
    bean thread
    thousand-year eggs.
I like Connie with her shorts sky-high,
pretend it doesn't matter if I die.

If anyone wants to know how it works
I can tell them:
    combustion
    corrosion
    pipe fittings
    the way trees fall

Inversion

Barry Ballard

It isn't difficult to imagine
the world turned upside down and waking
to frictionless sky, or pricking the skin
of our own imagination, breaking
the early vapors apart. What has it cost
the body's economy to distrust
compassion, to be suspicious in the stall
of an invisible river, to hush

our own brooding heart kneeling at its eroding
edge? Why shouldn't it be the weak balance
of the "ought" resting on its back, dreaming
the shape of clouds from concrete, or opposing
thermal currents lifting the map from our hands,
or stars in windows where the conscience is screened.

Midwest theodicy

Sean Lause

I hunger for this town that taught my bones.
I bite my wrists to drink the dreaming there.
Lima, Ohio, its streets my arteries,
my heart a factory, prisons in my eyes.
Summer of '68, Martians and Mansons,
blood dripping from each newspaper I tossed
across brown lawns, houses warped from thirst,
water sprinklers clicking diamonds in the sun,
velvet mosquitoes draining our lives
with the necessary needle of need.

Pumping my bike until my thighs quiver
like tender animals, as if the bike's breaths
depend on my search, searching for something,
something in the wonderball night, racing home
from the Ranger theater, heat lightning
illuminating monsters in the sky.
Home safe, probing shadows, scaring ghosts,
touching the silence in old bowls and spoons,
thirsty pine trees dusting a sleepy moon.

Daylight always came slaughtering children
as I lugged the fallen world up each street,
seeing through the eyes of the junk yard dog
strutting past dead buses and bleeding chevys.
Black man slung on a chair in a doorway,
his sunlit face worn and creased as his shoes,
radio blues, his house a busted skull.
Louise's Drug Store, five cents for water,
rusted ceiling fans swirling exhaustion,
"Nigger Baby" candies trapped in a jar.

Endless August, race riots, skies like bones,
cancer moon between abandoned buildings
like an old man creeping between tombstones,
swifts circling, cries striating the sky,
a bum stumbling to join two cigar butts,
young whores across from the police station,
the wind puffing their dresses pink and green,
Kewpee Burger, photos of cows on the wall,
Old Man Ganser clutching the back booth,
chanting tales of Iwo Jima to the floor.

Autumn rains came at last, whispering sweetness.
Blossoming into lightness at route's end,
I learned the art of invisibility,
seeking fleeting redemptions in the doom:
Father humming, spreading mayonnaise sandwich,
Mother in her yellow dress, reading Rimbaud,
bathing the porch in her light, like a firefly
cupped in palms, I lie gently in her lap.
She smooths my hair in silent benedictions
as swishtree apples thump the earth, my heart.

Acacias

Davide Trame

Breathing them in the ready lush new green
you get a gust of the continent where you, small,
loved their smell but didn't know their names
and now that you know them you really don't know
anything more
just the same ambrosial vein in the air
bringing back your marvelled child's stare
and the boundless space where to restart the tale you love more,
the maze of whispers in the wood you have never left,
the vast nearness still to explore.

House Wren

Jeanine Stevens

one without looks within
Thomas Hardy

Dusk, a bird at the window, intent jet eyes,
perfect circles—I look away, but somehow
she attaches to the sill above my desk.
Should I make a small sketch of barely
audible sounds and shadows before supper?

The darkening sky outlines leaves sharp
as beaks. Branches thick as arms scratch
eaves, dwarf the endless pecking—small dots
in exactly the same spot as if to poke through
and touch me. I'm puzzled, but know the signs,
omens, gifts, symbols in dream journals.

Is this how it happens? A spec of warm fluff,
the totem you hoped would be a fox, eagle,
at least a lunar moth, is just a simple house
wren you are smart enough to notice. I half
expect a key to peek from under the tiny wing.

Selected Works
by
Charles Wright

Jesuit Graves

Midsummer. Irish overcast. Oatmeal-colored sky.
The Jesuit pit. Last mass
For hundreds whose names are incised on the marble wall
Above the gravel and grassless dirt.
Just dirt and the small stones—
                            how strict, how self-effacing.

Not suited for you, however, Father Bird-of-Paradise,
Whose *plumage of far wonder* is not formless and not faceless,
Whatever you might have hoped for once.
Glasnevin Cemetery, Dublin, 3 July 1995.
For those who would rise to meet their work,
                            that work is scaffolding.

Sacrifice is the cause of ruin.
The absence of sacrifice is the cause of ruin.
Thus the legends instruct us,
North wind through the flat-leaved limbs of the sheltering trees,
Three desperate mounds in the small, square enclosure,
                    souls God-gulped and heaven-hidden.

P. Gerardus Hopkins, 28 July 1844—8 June 1889, Age 44.
And then the next name. And then the next,
Soldiers of misfortune, lock-step into a star-colored tight dissolve,
History's hand-me-ons. But you, Father Candescence,
You, Father Fire?
                Whatever rises comes together, they say. They say.

A Short History of the Shadow

Thanksgiving, dark of the moon.
Nothing down here in the underworld but vague shapes and black holes,
Heaven resplendent but virtual
Above me,
                trees stripped and triple-wired like Irish harps.
Lights on Pantops and Free Bridge mirror the eastern sky.
Under the bridge is the river,
                    the red Rivanna.
Under the river's redemption, it says in the book,
It says in the book,
Through water and fire the whole place becomes purified,
The visible by the visible, the hidden by what is hidden.

––––––––––

Each word, as someone once wrote, contains the universe.
The visible carries all the invisible on its back.
Tonight, in the unconditional, what moves in the long-limbed grasses,
                         what touches me
As though I didn't exist?
What is it that keeps moving,
                a tiny pillar of smoke
Erect on its hind legs,
              loose in the hollow grasses?
A word I don't know yet, a little word, containing infinity,
Noiseless and unrepentant, in sift through the dry grass.
Under the tongue is the utterance.
Under the utterance is the fire, and then the only end of fire.

––––––––––

Only Dante, in Purgatory, casts a shadow,
L'ombra della carne, the shadow of flesh—

                                  everyone else *is* one.
The darkness that flows from the world's body, gloomy spot,
Pre-dogs our footsteps, and follows us,

                            diaphanous bodies
Watching the nouns circle, and watching the verbs circle,
Till one of them enters the left ear and becomes a shadow
Itself, sweet word in the unwaxed ear.
This is a short history of the shadow, one part of us that's real.
This is the way the world looks
In late November,

          no leaves on the trees, no ledge to foil the lightfall.

No ledge in early December either, and no ice,
La Niña unhosing the heat pump

                    up from the Gulf,
Orange Crush sunset over the Blue Ridge,
No shadow from anything as evening gathers its objects
And eases into earshot.
Under the influx the outtake,

                Leon Battista Alberti says,
Some lights are from stars, some from the sun
And moon, and other lights are from fires.
The light from the stars makes the shadow equal to the body.
Light from fire makes it greater,

           there, under the tongue, there, under the utterance.

Thinking of Marsilio Ficino at
The First Hint of Autumn

We yo-yo the Absolute big-time,
Dark little spinning thing.
                              Still, death is the deeper exile and
Waits for our fancy—
Its business is process, and hiding out, and keeping in touch,
Tenth night in a row of rain,
Black as an owl's eye,
Thunder and lightening out of the West Virginia mountains like God's yips
And hotfoots,
                    trees processional maidens dipping in turn,
Cold front from the north
Pinning our ears back, shorting our breath.

Last night and a world away.
This afternoon like a waffle, indented and warm,
Delicious and blue on the tongue,
                                    early September.
Ficino, however, is probably right, the Absolute
Not being an exile but a grace,
And waits for no one,
                            the way, this afternoon, the sun
Kindles and plumps the dogwood berries,
The way the individual necks in the cutting garden
Bow dutifully to what's to come,
The way Orion and the Pleiades
                            rise up, ready to go on.

Via Negativa

If a man wants to be sure of his road,
he must close his eyes and walk in the dark.

St. John of the Cross

In southwest Virginia, just this side of Abingdon,
The mountains begin to shoulder up,
The dogwoods go red and leaf-darkened,
And leftover roadside wildflowers neon among the greens—
Early October, and Appalachia dyes her hair.
What is it about the southern mountains
                                    that vacuums me out,
That seems to hold me on an invisible flame until I rise up and veer
weightless and unrepentant?
The great valley pours into Tennessee, the ridges like epaulets
To the north, landscape in pinks-and-greens
                                    off to the south.

———————

How pretty to think that gods abound,
                              and everything stays forgotten,
That words are dust, and everyone's lip that uttered them is dust,
Our line of discomfort inalterable, sun-struck,
From not-ness into not-ness,
Our prayers—like raiment, like char scraps— rising without us,
Into an everlasting,
                    which goes on without us,
Blue into blue into blue—
Our prayers, like wet-wrung pieces of glass,
Surf-spun, unedged and indestructible and shining,

Our lives a scratch on the sky,

                            painless, beyond recall.

I never remember going out at night, full moon,
Stalking the yard in California the way I do here,
First frost
          starting to sort its crystals out, moon shadows
Tepid and underslung on the lawn.
I don't remember—although I should—the emptiness
That cold brings, and stillness brings.
I never remember remembering the odd way
Evergreens have in night light

                         of looming and floating,
The way the spirit, leaving your mouth, looms too and floats
In front of you like breath,
               leading the way as it disappears in the darkness.

Long journey, short road, the saying goes,
Meaning our lives,
             meaning the afterlife of our nights and days
During our sleepwalk through them.
The verbal hunger, the narrowness
Between the thing itself and the naming of the thing
Coils like a tapeworm inside us
              and waits to be filled.
Our lives continue on course, and reject all meaning,
Each of us needing his martyrdom,
             each of us needing that hard love.
We sink to our knees like Sunday, we rise and we sink again.
There is no pardon for this.

Bottomless water, heart's glass.
Each year the autumn comes that was not supposed to be
Back in the garden without language,
Each year, dead leaves like words
                              falling about our shoulders,
Each year, same words, same flash and gold guise.
So be it. The Angel of the Serpent That Never Arrives
Never arrives, the gates stay shut
                              under a shine and a timelessness.
On Locust Avenue the fall's fire
Collapses across the lawn,
The trees bear up their ruin,
            and everything nudges our lives toward the coming ash.

There Is a Balm in Gilead

Crows in a caterwaul on the limb-laced edge of the afternoon,
Three scored like black notes in the bare oak across the street.
The past is a thousand-mile view I can't quite see the end of.
Heart-halved, I stare out the window to ease its medicine in.

———————

Landscape's a local affliction that has no beginning and no end,
Here when we come and here when we go.
Like white clouds, our poems drift over it,
                                        looking for somewhere to lie low.
They neither hinder nor help.

———————

Night sky black water,
                    reservoir crow-black and sky-black,
Starless and Godless.
Cars trundle like glowworms across the bridge, angel-eyed,
Silver-grilled.
                The fish in the waters of heaven gleam like knives.

———————

I write, as I said before, to untie myself, to stand clear,
To extricate an absence,
The ultimate hush of language,
                        (fricative, verb, and phoneme),
The silence that turns the silence off.

———————

Butt-end of January, leaf-ash and unclaimed snow,
Cold blue of blue jay cutting down to the feeder box,
The morning lit with regret,
No trace of our coming, no trace of our going back.

Homage to Mark Rothko

I tried their ways for a little while,
But wasn't at ease with them, they
$\qquad$ not bringing me to the revealed.
Still, I kept on praising them.
I cast my body upon the earth.
I cast my body upon the waters,
$\qquad$ and kept on praising them all.
The glories refused to shelter me,
Nothing explained, nothing brought to bear.
I tried their ways for a little while,
$\qquad$ but nothing was ever revealed.

———————

We enter the fields of memory and devotion.
Allow me, as Paul Celan says,
$\qquad$ to thank you from there—
Landscape, this world, this poor earth
Under the sun, holding nothing back,
This almost-nature that goes from light to light, that melts
The gold coin between our teeth,
That raises, like water, the shadow of the wound
$\qquad$ up to our necks.
Allow me to thank you from all the language there is in that.

Early December, autumn's ragtag and cockamamie end.
Next door, Doctor Dave's got his pickup truck at the raked leaf
$\qquad$ pile,
Bird feeders float like flying saucers
$\qquad$ suddenly through the trees,

Plaster Madonna and wood-cut edge of the Blue Ridge
Zoomed in by the bare branches.
Turkey buzzards and crows

                        drifting like lint on the Piedmont sky,
December, ragtag and gypsy day.
Allow me to thank you from all that's missing in all of that.

Form cannot deconstruct or be annihilated, you said.
The communion of saints,

                        desire and its aftermath,
Chalice and chasuble, bread and wine—
Just sonar of purification, imprints,

                                pretty tomfoolery.
Whatever *it* is, it's beyond all this, you said.

                        And painting and language and music.
Stars are the first pages, you said, in The Book of Unknowing.
Behind them are all the rest.
Form is eternal and exists unwreckable, past repair, you said.

———————————

In the light that shines without shadow,

                            our hiding place.
Comfort metastasizes.
Wintering in. Wintering in to distance and wordlessness.
Comfort blackens the X rays.

                      Echoes, deep subtractions.
Wretched the body dependent upon the body.
Wretched the flesh and the soul therein.
I tried to give form to the formless,

                      and speech to the unspeakable.
To the light that shines without shadow, I gave myself.

Doppelganger

Blank page, old friend, what do you say now
After all these years of runes,
>   tight lips and tighter lids?
You get more attention than sex does
From your acolytes, and still hold your tongue,
Phantom limb, inscrutable dog
>   fast asleep in a white light.

Such waxed looks and wan, such silences.

Small Galaxies

by
Edward A. Dougherty

Power of Poetry — *A Celebration*
BERKELEY, CALIFORNIA
2004

Contents

The ground of the soul is dark.
                                        Meister Eckhart

One should identify oneself with the universe itself.
                                        Simon Weil

Setting Out

Beginnings have their own success

like snowfall: the clarity that something
is finally moving. This time

it's you. Are you drawn
by a more promising field, or squeezed
until leaving is the only way
to stay whole? Maybe

you've cracked open,
growing too large for old forms,
growing even now
in the white heart of winter.

In any case, you stand shaking
in the momentous world.
A black-capped chickadee
navigates the crab-apples' tangle
to land and feed:

do you believe in birds only
when they are visible? The white snow
is a kind of emptiness

you fully understand.

A Room Full of Expectation

In the winter, when snow fell by the foot, there was dancing in this room. Laughing circles. Legs and arms, music and languages from many countries all going around and around while the world outside managed itself as it always does. This is a roomful of breathing. A cargo of expectation. It would be easy to say simple things like, "Half is lit but the whole is in the Light," but darkness, like these whitewashed bricks, surrounds us.

Once we were asked to recall exemplars, and the stories made the room swell with all those invisible ones who have urged us on to this moment. The father in the front of the boat, holding steady. An old woman who went out to share in the gathering so she wouldn't die in her hogan, saving the family the burden of burning it to the ground. A writer working in fits and starts between child tending and dozing off in the vast, silent sanctuaries after midnight, and her book contains a truth that now lives in one of us all these years later. The friend whose very life was a comfort, even when he himself didn't know it. These spirits gathered in this bare room as they always do; not speaking is only one part of our response.

In candlelight the walls seemed softer, more like a body than a building, and here we were living inside it. The sitting and breathing together became part of that larger life. This is always true, of course, but that night, another part of us woke up to it. A space opened in us, as wisdom does. We were living in our larger self, and a small white room was breathing inside us.

Taizé

Taizé is a river valley breaking into all the shades of green to bear witness to the power of greening. Taizé is a gathering of people, an abbey, a movement. It is a way of prayer. It is a flock of birds all moving as one, all heading to a place they know by feel. Each voice begins by gathering air, soul, soil. In this drawing in, there is France and England, the States and Germany, Argentina and Laos. There is a steppe with sweetgrass growing waist high, smelling like rain. There is a mountain slope so steep and cragged that it is no longer beautiful but it is beautiful. Taizé is a line of poplars, unmoving and swaying, so green they are black from a distance. And Taizé is the first single voice lifting out from the trees and the rest of the flock, rising to fly through the radiant, green valley.

Lucy's Message

She rose slowly. She's been crying
or will be soon. On the window ledge,

the glass vase is gray-green
from dust and years of holding water.

She grasps it around the lip.
See? she says, holding it before us:

a tangle of winter sticks
with a few tan leaves

left from a distant season.
See? A single white blossom.

The promise of the earth.
And she places it in our midst.

Into Darkness

I. Descent
Sometimes when I am breathing carefully, not taking for granted the complexities of that filling and emptying, how molecule by invisible molecule I touch the cottonwood tree quivering in the breeze, sometimes I feel a descent. I sink into an image of darkness. I descend into soil. *God saw that the light was good and God separated the light from the darkness* because the darkness was already with God. Like breath, it didn't need to be created—both were in God before the beginning. My breathing is sometimes like this, a trail I follow, a river path after flash flooding: willow and brush all tangled and crossed, all pointing in the direction of water's flow. I follow this breathing, this thin strand that comes out of my body and connects me to the world. I think of Beth's cornflower seeds, which breathe even in the dark of their packets at the store. Though they need light, the seeds would burn up if we threw them into the sun, but hidden in the soil, separated from the light, they sprout. They emerge like hands, heels together, palms up ready to catch moisture, light, and the whole breathing world, to funnel it down into the roots, just beginning to reach out. Sometimes when I am breathing carefully, this is what I am.

II. Only This
In the beginning there was no time
and nothing to measure it with
there was only this

Darkness   closed in around itself
wonderful and perfect

In the darkness there was breathing
it moved through the dark
part darkness and part breath

In the breathing there were waters
over which the breath moved

In the waters there was no violence
as creation had not begun
there was motion but no matter

In the beginning there was radiation
moving in all directions at once

III. On the Trinity

"The effects could be called
unprecedented,
magnificent, beautiful, stupendous,

and terrifying. The whole country

was lighted by a searing light
with the intensity many times
that of the midday sun. It was golden,

purple, violet, gray, and blue.

First the air blast pressed hard against people,
to be followed almost immediately
by the strong, sustained awesome

roar which warned of doomsday

and made us feel we puny things
were blasphemous
to dare tamper with the forces

heretofore reserved for the Almighty."

(General Farrell, Deputy to Manhattan
Project Commander General Leslie
Groves: On the Trinity Test, July 16, 1945)

Fishing Boats on the Beach
after van Gogh

Crimson like roses. Like our lives,
they are outlined in black, deep and impenetrable.
Blue oars to dip into water
when winds fail. Like the sun
crowning the horizon, these boats
carry such promise. They seem to smile,
filled with something that makes them
settle into the sand. I think of Jesus

in the tossing prow
while wild animals took up the shape
of the sea. He said his friends
were of little faith, believing so much
in the logic of nature,
of what is most visible.

He rose, spoke to the water and wind,
and they lay down to sleep,
contented. Night gathered around the boat,
leaving the men to wonder
which promise to believe.

Sequoias

Like sisters who gather over coffee because one of them has found a lump in her breast, these three redwoods are straggled and lovely. A lost species growing right here in suburbia. Sometimes you have to go all the way to China—which they did to "discover" these trees—to find that beauty, that rough elegance that's within the whole time. All winter, hanging in their high branches, tangled in their hair: Venus, that evening star which is not a star but a planet whose features are all named for women. It has something to do with endurance, which for most of us would be enough. There's a certain grace in having things named appropriately: redwood/redbud, tree/ tumor, malignant/benign. Where branches pushed out of the trunk, a kind of teardrop crevice formed, as if growing in one place takes something from somewhere else. That's why standing together makes all the difference. Over the years, the moon whitewashes everything with romance, but the sisters endure. April comes again and the redwoods put out tiny, soft needles like green fans.

Resistance

I've met many who looked up into that clear blue August sky. I've
seen the evidence. A lip drooped into a kind of sadness. A curl
of hair to hide the cheek plowed by surgeries. Half an ear.
I lived in a house that didn't burn in the bomb's incredible confla-
gration, a house that was a post office before the war, a house
that put up soldiers before they surged out from Ujina & into
the killing fields of Asia & the Pacific, a house that sparrows
recognized as home.
In that house, a man showed slides about Vietnam just after the
embargo was lifted—he narrates: Usually a third person
negotiates the price & takes the money, but eventually she did
sell me her jacket. The man in the hat is wearing pajamas. The
woman on the right was for sale.
Those are missiles.
If you want to stop the course of armaments, the monk tells me,
you have to resist. Begin by resisting in your own life. It's been
a long road, & then I lived in Hiroshima. Shall we discuss the
suffering of war? Start with your pain or mine?
In Vietnam, the man told us, the people eat noodles every day.
Children play on the missiles that point into Asian clouds.
The world is a small struggle.
It begins with a woman crazy with loneliness who needs to feel
like she's running the show, no matter what. And at every step
she's suffered. Sometimes she'd thank me for some cour-
tesy—I swear I've never felt such a stab. Sorrow's the only
vehicle left that will carry her words.
Meanwhile, tanks roll into another city & newspapers have always
been full of war. In places I cannot pronounce, schoolgirls
look into the sky asking how to resist this rain. They ask who
made this unhappiness, when will it go away.
One woman said it's just human nature to be brutal. A man told me
the Jews started the war. It was the United States & other
Western imperial/colonial powers which forced Japan to
liberate Asia.
A high school student told me *history's a sleeping pill.* He prefers
rock music from England. Says his grades are poor, but he
hopes for college because the world is becoming slices of

49

light—college, he says, is the only way. But it's a long road. He
says for the next year he must study each day late into the night
just to take the test. History, how will that help?

And I remember the man in sturdy glasses who told about lying
about his age so he could run away & join the army. All he
wanted to do was his duty to God & country, all he wanted was
the honor to die, but—before that honor—he wanted to kill as
many of the enemy as he could. Instead, he was assigned to the
secret unit developing a new weapon, one that would strike fear
into your bones if you knew of it.

Does it matter if he was Vietnamese or French, German or Japanese?
Does it matter if he was American?

All I know is that the atomic bomb was dropped on a inhabited city
just 21 days after its first test.

I know that everyone has a reason to kill but not everyone does, & I
know that I lived in a wooden house that escaped the fires, & it
swayed like a mother cradling her infant.

Saucer Magnolia

Pink was never a soft, girlie-girlie color to these trees, but life-
and-death. Beauty's a matter of survival. Someone said we take all
the wrong things seriously, and this is one of them. I want to say
something so we won't deny such power even though most words
blow away soon after falling to the ground. I am dying a little
with every blossom. A group of us stretched out on the grass
before the thick petals began raining down and read Mark's
Gospel aloud, hearing in human voices our own harshness, stupid-
ity, and possibility. The sky's always been this blue. Daffodils,
tulips, cherry trees always break into beauty after winter. I am
becoming something, but I can't know what yet.

Saint John

It's not fever, but a heat,
a burning, not quite
the Urakami conflagration,
but still I cannot drift

into night's deep sway.
Candles swallowed
by a wolf.
The names of the dead.

Kathy Feher once told me,
You are like
the Beloved Disciple.
The same tenderness.

Living water, bread
of life, vine and branches—
these are all
John's names

for the fire in his bones.
Others' pain became
his faithful companion.
He died, not of torture,

but of old age, his heart
finally giving out, face upturned
to the bright
Nagasaki light.

Long Pilgrimage

Like in any other dining hall, the usual rectangular tables, surrounded by wooden chairs, are the setting for familiar customs of sharing food. Between meals, though, the room holds a strange repose, a quiet like my schooldays' kitchen after the dishwasher was finished churning. I'd spread my books across the table to do my homework while another part of me stared from the night-blank windows. Those were the days I learned that *the longest journey is the journey inwards.* I think of the prophet, Elijah, running off to Mount Sinai when the king wanted to kill him. On foot, he traveled days through the wilderness to finally fling himself, exhausted, on the hard ground where he slept. An angel woke him, and by his head Elijah found bread and a jar of water. "It will be a long journey," the angel told him. He ate and fell asleep again. A second time, the angel woke him up with the same message, the same gifts. Because his life's at stake, he did as he's told. Elijah was renewed enough to climb the sacred mountain and face the God of the Universe, who sweeps by in the small whispering sound. The dining room is dedicated to such long pilgrimages, to such transformations. How the leaves of spinach or lettuce grow eyes in us. Olives, crushed to oil and sent across the ocean, gain legs and, in us, walk the earth. At mealtimes, the dining space fills with motion and randomness. People with trays head for the side table for drinks or scan faces for that sign of hospitality. Glad to be useful, plates and glasses and silver are unafraid to make sound. Each table becomes a small galaxy. Each of us is made from elements issued from stars that collapsed so intensely that their fundamental nature changed.

Bartimaeus
(Mark 10:46-52)

Stone chips and pebbles
speckle the low mud wall.

Only a few hours of shade
before the summer sun
blisters and brazes his skin.

Sound of the crowd reaches him
long before any dust
or condemnation.

He could see once,
hold a job, have a place
in the circles
of economy, socializing,
and the rest.

Why cry out first
for pity? Attention?
Being recognized
as a human being?

There's no suspense here:
we know Jesus
restores his sight.
But before that,

in the haze of dust, the stink
of hot bodies
stalled beside an earthen wall,

there is this stark moment—

What do you want me
to do for you?

Opening

The doors blow ajar and we all
turn to face the space
opening. This voice

will not be shouted down,
will not be argued away.

Push the chairs back, add another
to our circle. The doors
have blown open; something holy

has entered the room: nothing
will be the same.

For Mtoto

Your eyes, Child, are dark waters, still and deep. They receive the sky as it collapses into us, receive the green trees as they leaf out into towering beings guarding us all. Your eyes take us in. For a year now you've shifted from hip to hip, from one stranger to another and you will not remember us. We've passed through you like a fragrance. But you, Child, you who watched us, who drew from us our desire to delight, you have become something sure and firm in us. You have been carried off to New Zealand where the sea whispers a lullaby all day and long into the night. Child, you have been taken away to Europe where there are castles and cities like every other city, but you, alert and watchful, have been slipped into a small country of silence. You've been carried into the mountains of South America where the air becomes so thin people gasp for it like love, where the soil slips to the sea and you, Child, will watch this migration. Can I say you are the body of Christ taken whole and understood only in part, understood in as many ways as you are taken. In us you are always young, Child. But in you, we have passed through like rain, and anything you remember will have to be given to you again by someone else. We who pass like shadows on the wall remember you as you grow up in a place we cannot imagine. But we imagine you there.

Woodchip Path

Sometimes when walking the path along the southeast, you can't tell what's traffic and what's wind in the needles. Mostly it's the highway, newly laid down but laid out in minds and meetings for decades. In the time between decision and dynamite, green spaces throughout the area slipped away, and are now like the faces of the dead which are so familiar and so lost. There are times when tears come burning: the mind suddenly grasps how far away these lovers have moved. The heart has always understood this distance. Mostly, though, it's a sound like the surf, a sighing in the spruce trees, a moan in the pines. One day a woodchuck lumbering across, all fur and wobble as it tried to escape. A few days before, the rain had pounded down, briefly and completely. The water had carved a rivulet in the path as it pushed the chips aside or carried them down the hill, where the woodchuck was now heading. At night, when leaving the open Firbank Field and entering the embrace of trees planted by men who refused to go to war, the sky collapses under the canopy of branches and sticks and is as far away as surf pounding the shore. Woodchips piled by the cartload cannot cover up the beating pulse of the earth under our feet. The chips themselves contain a spark of the trees which once knew the vitality of the soil. The heart understands this; that's why the path takes such care and so much work. Each step is a memorial to what is passing, to what is past. Each step is a leaving behind and an arrival.

The Craft Studio

The wheels spin like my mind in silence. Paper remembers the flow of sap, exchange of sunlight into sugar. The tables are high, closer to the heart. Another room dedicated to transformation. Clay becomes plates and bowls and shapes it takes two hands to discover. Once I lost myself in mixing colors, slipping into each other, becoming new shades. Watercolors are like tears in a still puddle, like sunrise, like the secret gestures of incense. The paint floated and mixed as if it forgot who it was and only when the soggy card stock dried did the pigment come to its senses. Isn't this what we do when we fall in love? When we learn about a Florida town in 1996 that has one bathroom for Blacks and one for Whites? This is the necessity of the Craft Studio. Vivaldi or Albinoni giving rhythm to the whole room, the large windows, the looms idly dreaming of streams of wool, the shelves hoarding their unfinished projects. What happens when a person gets lost in the shaping of material? All I know is that there is an emptying that comes with creation, a forgetting which must be acted out, a magnetic orientation that spins you around sometimes until you're pointing in the right direction.

Observing Silence (Return to August 6)

I was listening to other things,
eyes closed for other sight.
The cicadas had stopped.

The superfortress has been up there for hours
heading this way. The war has been over for years.

At the news, each member of the family, starting
with grandfather, rose and reached for the other.
Holding hands, they observed

Silence. Listening for other things.
My eyes were closed but I could see.

Clinging to bark, the cicadas had stopped.
A great thrumming of engines
filled the heavy chamber of a still summer evening.

Why return to this approaching? Why let years
circle like a stunned family? I have no answer but

Silence like a kind of listening. The world
and all its paces tuned to a pitch
just out of reach, a band of color just out of range.

Fireflies in the Bamboo Grove

The cicadas were still
grinding away the afternoon.
A single one would do it.

Slender poles in the wind.
The pond a shadow.
Invisibly, water eased itself
into that dark bowl.
Lilies were dull sticks, knobbed
where blossoms once were.

Every day this summer
green ran away, abandoning us like this.
Then, yellow lights in that hollow—
so much, so lively. And out of that motion,

A lightness came

Up out of the grasses that had turned black
in the night, out from the arching bamboo itself.

Eclipse

What is this we call sin? Is it like Morning Glory vining through the garden, the plant you spend hours ripping out and still it is all you see, tangling everywhere and undesirable?

The eclipsed moon rose over the line of pines, over the garden and Firbank Field. We huddled together pointing out the Dog Star, took the Pleiades eye-test, and watched as the moon changed from a rose in the black sky back to its familiar face. The night was soft around us as March blew through into April.

And belief? Is faith drawing connections in the scattered and distant stars whose light comes to us only later? Now a bear, now a mother and child. Is it a map we hold to the night sky to seek the shapes that are out there whether we recognize them yet or not?

We sang all the moon-songs we could remember, raising our voices with all the romantics who've gone before: heads tipped back to that white disk floating in the world beyond, the world above, the world all around us. And I, too, return again and again to it, finding it in the square of window facing east.

And I keep coming back, circling, revisiting the face of the mind that rounds and wanes like the moon which rose red and filled like a bowl with milk. *God is a mother,* someone once said, *who gives us the universe to suckle.*

How Ants Felled Two Trees

Before the circling wind let loose
its hungry pack of dogs

Before the rain weighed everything down with grief

Before the upper-atmosphere currents
aligned themselves
for acrimonious stillness

Before summer became what it is

There were ants

Black and numerous like drops of blood, like omens,
ants following the invisible trails
laid down by the bodies of their fellow ants
to the exposed heart of the sweetgum tree.

Each creature took only what it could bear,
no more and no less.

I don't know how the bark
was opened, but it was enough.

And before the ants,
before that engineered line of thieves,
there was a fragrance, a sweetness
going out into the world.

ABOUT THE AUTHORS

Edward A. Dougherty

After finishing his MFA in Creative Writing in Bowling Green, Ohio, Dougherty taught and tutored at the University and was poetry editor of the *Mid-American Review*. In 1993, he and his spouse went to Hiroshima to be volunteer directors of the World Friendship Center where they witnessed the fiftieth anniversary of the end of World War II and the atomic bombings. Upon their return, they spent eight months at the Quaker center for study and contemplation, Pendle Hill, where most of these poems originated. His chapbook, *The Metal of My Mouth,* was published by FootHills Publishing in April 2004. They live and work in Corning, where three rivers join in the hills of upstate New York.

Charles Wright

A native of the South, Charles Wright has published numerous collections of poetry. His recent works include: *Buffalo Yoga* (Farrar, Straus & Giroux, 2004), *Negative Blue* (2000); *Appalachia* (1998); and *Black Zodiac* (1997), which won the Pulitzer Prize and the *Los Angeles Times* Book Prize. In 1999 he was elected a Chancellor of the Academy of American Poets. Currently, he is the Souder Family Professor of English at the University of Virginia in Charlottesville.

✳